FINDINGS

SOCIETY OF FRIENDS
Armscote Old Meeting House
1680
Unused now except for a Meeting on
the 1st SUNDAY in every AUGUST
NOTICES

FINDINGS

An Enquiry into Quaker Religious Experience

ഌ ❀ ‍ઝ

edited by

Jack H. Wallis

QUAKER HOME SERVICE
•LONDON•

First published November 1993
by Quaker Home Service

ISBN 0 85245 251 9

CONTENTS

Know one another in that which is Eternal.

GEORGE FOX

The living Spirit grows and even outgrows
its earlier forms of expression.

C. G. JUNG

Try to live so that you can respond to that
of God in those you meet, and in yourself.

QUESTIONS & COUNSEL

ACKNOWLEDGEMENTS

The idea of making this enquiry originated from the pioneer work of The Alister Hardy Research Centre, described in two books reviewed in *The Friend**.

In scale and method, however, this enquiry is different although the aim is similar: to widen and deepen an understanding of religious (or spiritual) experience from the first-hand evidence of contributors.

The scope of the AHRC research was publicly announced and was unrestricted, extending over about twenty years. Some 5,000 replies were scientifically analysed, latterly using modern computer-based technology. By contrast, the contributors to this small-scale project are all Quakers (either Friends or Attenders) and part of the enquiry is concerned with whatever links there may be between Quaker membership and practice, and their own inner religious experience.

With such a very small and self-selected group systematic statistical analysis is not applicable. An appropriate procedure had to be devised. I warmly acknowledge the help, support and expertise of a Support Group with whose guidance the form and method of this project were planned.

The Support Group consisted of: Dr W. A. Allchin, Jo Farrow, David Firth, Dr David Hay, Ralph Hetherington, Jim Pym and John Withrington, to all of whom I offer appreciation and thanks for their help.

Thanks are also due to Friends in special interest groups of London Yearly Meeting, particularly the Universalists and the Seekers Association who kindly sent me helpful material at the planning stage.

Soon after this project began I heard of a piece of research undertaken by Jean Dundas in 1967-68. She worked for a year at Woodbrooke at a painstaking study of religious

*Seeing the Invisible by Meg Maxwell and Verena Tschudin, Arkana 1990 and *Religious Experience Today* by David Hay (author of *Exploring Inner Space*, and former Director of AHRC), Mowbray 1990.

experience among Quakers. It was based mainly on testimonies, articles and letters published in *The Friend*. She included some accounts of experiences from individual Friends, including some who attended the World Conference in 1967. Jean Dundas kindly gave me access to her unpublished material, for which I am most grateful.

I would also like to express my gratitude to Polly Tatum, former Publications Secretary of QSRE, for allowing the reproduction, in black and white, of some of her collection of over 900 slides of Quaker places. Travelling to take these photographs was a spiritual journey in itself, and her pictures compliment the text beautifully.

Special acknowledgements and thanks are, of course, due to the contributors who supplied the essential material quoted in these pages. Without their ready participation the enquiry would have foundered. It has been a privilege to be entrusted with their experiences. The handling of such sensitive material has not been easy and may, in a few instances, be individually disappointing. This is a vocational risk for any editor but if it has occurred I much regret it.

Warm thanks are also due to Jenny Dixon for kindly sending the poem printed at the end of the text. Her words surely catch the special atmosphere of a Quaker Meeting for Worship as only a poet's can.

J.H.W.

BACKGROUND TO THE ENQUIRY

This small-scale enquiry is offered for anyone interested in religious or spiritual experience, whether or not they are Quaker. It was originally suggested in an article in *The Friend* which invited any Quaker or regular Attender to send for details of the project. Fifty-three applied and a copy of the leaflet sent to each of them is attached at *Appendix A*. Twenty-nine people took part in the enquiry, though not all in all of it. The third and fourth questions (in *Part II*) were sent out some eight weeks after the first two.

The questions put to each contributor are placed at the head of each section of the relevant replies. The order of replies in each section is different.

Subjects as comprehensive and strongly-felt as are politics, sex and religion are tricky to enquire into because one can inadvertently influence replies by the way the questions are worded. It is therefore as well to explain how this project was planned and what were the principles behind it.

Religion can be said to have an outside and an inside. The outside includes general matters of theology, history, tradition as well as formal questions of organisation, administration, buildings, vestments and furnishings. It also includes forms of service, creeds, ritual and liturgy. By contrast, the inner side consists of each individual's conviction, faith and religious or spiritual experience.

Religion may thus be treated as an inner and personal event or as an impersonal, objective study.

The first part of this enquiry is concerned only with the inner, personal aspect. It is based on the opinions and experience of each Quaker or Attender who replied and they write in their own words.

All volunteered to take part. With so small a number, the replies should not be regarded as typical, either individually or collectively. Moreover, the experiences described in *Part I* and *II* are so individual, spontaneous and subjective that it would be unwise to attempt to classify or analyse them.

Part III is more concerned with outer aspects of religion, so far as it deals with the Quaker way of worship and the influence this may (or may not) have on the spiritual life of those who attend; the experience is inner and subjective, but the form of worship is general and, indeed, traditional.

Brief comments are included after each section to help in continuity. *Appendix B* gives further editorial detail.

The questions sent to contributors were as follows:

1   *From your own personal experience, what do you understand by religious (or spiritual) experience ?*

2   *Can you describe a religious (or spiritual) experience that has happened to yourself (more than one if you like)?*

3   *Is your own religious (or spiritual) experience specially linked to your being a Quaker (or Attender) ? If so, please enlarge.*

4   *Does attending Quaker Meeting for Worship encourage or discourage, hinder or help you in relation to religious (or spiritual) experience ?*

The first two questions were included in Notes describing the project which were sent to those who applied for them. (See *Appendix A*). The other two were sent about two months later.

౪

PART I

MEANINGS

Introduction

Quakers tend to be practical people who try to relieve and improve the lot of their fellow-beings, without distinction other than need. So, of course, do legions of others whether religious or not, whether Christian or not, who are motivated by goodwill and imaginative and energetic compassion. One has only to consider the extent of voluntary and charitable work, here and worldwide, and also the multitudes of people employed by statutory departments and the professions all concerned with the prevention and relief of distress and suffering, persecution and injustice, to appreciate how widespread are the practical efforts of men and women to promote the well-being of their fellows and relieve hardship. Most of these vocations used to have a religious origin.

Today it is clearly impossible to know how many of these people derive their compassionate activity wholly or partly from religion, either directly or remotely. For Quakers, the link is conscious and deliberate as proclaimed in their formal name, *The Religious Society of Friends*. As is well-known, their particular way of worship is an unstructured meeting, based on silence and directed towards the spiritual basis of life as the mainspring of goodwill. All the same, each such meeting is routinely followed by considering events and activities locally, nationally and worldwide.

The Meeting for Worship is at the heart of the Quaker way of life. It is a determined effort to link practical concerns with the religious and spiritual experience that informs and inspires them. This last aspect is the primary subject of this enquiry, so that we can 'enter imaginatively into other people's experience'. How can that be done?

Religious or spiritual experience is at once so vivid and individual and yet, to many people, so familiar as to be instantly recognizable. But it remains virtually indefinable.

In a covering letter, one contributor wrote, 'What seemed such a major event for me seems such a non-event when written-down'. This wistful little comment emphasises the difficulty of putting into words a religious or spiritual experience. Unless one is a poet, one can hardly find words to recapture the essential intensity or lustre. We seem to lack an adequate vocabulary and are obliged to hunt for symbols or mataphors or fall back upon technical or emotional language.

Competent and gifted artists or poets often achieve a truly articulate expression of spiritual matters. Their vocation and skill enable them to reach an extra dimension of experience in whatever medium their talent finds expression. But one could hardly expect contributors to reply in poetry, though one did.* The same struggle to find adequate words is familiar to Quakers from Meeting for Worship, when the urge to 'minister' becomes so strong as to get a member standing and trying.

The questions in *Part III* and *Part IV* were framed so as to stimulate just such a spontaneous response.

* Jenny Dixon. See page 95

Replies to First Question

From your own personal experience, what do you understand by religious (or spiritual) experience ?

A Higher Power

What I understand by religious (or spiritual) experience is a sense of relationship with a Higher Power or Spirit to which I can look for guidance and support, and which can also give me a sense of unity with other living things, especially fellow humans but animal and plant life too - and even perhaps inanimate nature.

I think there is also probably communion with spirits - and I do not mean Spiritualism but the companionship of loved ones no longer on this earth, and the kind of communion one can have with writers, artists, musicians through their works, whether they are alive or dead.

I would probably speak of Religious rather than Spiritual experience if it related to a particular faith.

Personal and Particular

My experience is very limited but very important to me. I am sure it has much in common with the experience of everyone else.

In all conscious thought there is a stream of disjointed facts,concepts and feelings which can by an effort of will organise into something coherent, something that can result in action. Most of this activity is very familiar to us. It is something that we recognise as personal and particular to ourselves.

But on occasions some thought or feeling intrudes into our consciousness which, because of its superior quality to our own thoughts, we can call religious or spiritual. This quality is of great variety and has the characteristic that it comes in its own time and is usually unbidden. It is usually good, in the sense that it encourages our spiritual growth. But some unconscious thought, by a promise of short-term gain, can direct us in the wrong way resulting in a set-back in growth and the negative feelings of guilt and despair.

Another characteristic of superior thoughts is the feeling of tremendous controlled power and gentleness that they engender. They match but never overwhelm our capabilities to understand. On the other hand they invite a response which seems to be limitless.

LIVING IN THE MYSTERY

By religious or spiritual experience I mean moments or times of awareness when one is in contact with some other realm of consciousness. The essence of the experience is wordless.

To me such experiences are the most important and valuable thing there is. Apart from the almost daily recurring moments of wonder and uplift, I have not had a great many such experiences. Meeting for Worship is for me an extraordinarily powerful forum for such heightened awareness.

I suppose that religious or spiritual experience is, to me, a matter of living in the mystery. The experiences go beyond the intellect and normal perception.

HEAVENLY BABY

The word spiritual for me describes a vital dimension of life, consciousness of which is not confined to, or by, religion. My personal experiences of this dimension vary enormously and range from a sense of being blessed when, for instance, I am receiving healing; a sense of linking up with my whole self which is wiser than my everyday self; and so on in variety to one or two experiences of enough intensity to bring about changes in my life.

Some dreams in technicolour could, I suppose, qualify as spiritual experiences - the kind of dream from which I awake with a sense of wonder and even joy - not as often as I would wish. In such dreams I am conscious of flying as if this were a natural accomplishment; the light everywhere is unique and recognised as normal illumination for these experiences.

Lately, I dream about a 'heavenly baby' - more beautiful than any I have met in life, so the word heavenly is unavoidable.

SOMETHING ELSE

By a 'religious or spiritual experience' I understand a sense of 'something else'. It is a strong impression that there is something or someone in a place beyond and above and transcendent over what I perceive with either the intellect or the five senses.

It is a something that is wholesome and good to experience, and something that transforms my mood and my perception. I use the word 'place' because in my own life religious experience has often been associated with particular places. To me that is relevant, though I don't entirely understand why.

A CIRCLE OF LIGHT

It was in 1958 that it was clear to me that a gift I had could be woven into the pattern of life. From the time I was about 11 I realised that I saw things that others did not, and knew that something would come about long before it did - thoughts would come into my mind which I dismissed as fanciful.

It has not been an easy gift, for I know what people around me are thinking and have tested it often and proved it to be so. Let me call it 'heightened intuition'.

Coincidences and right timings began to happen to a degree that was almost laughable, both in small and large activities.

I have learned a technique for transforming negative thoughts; one should think the Lord's Prayer, to clear the line as it were, then a circle of Light with a crucifix in it and into this circle I put not only negative thoughts but people in trouble and leave it. People in trouble could be close friends or passers-by. I have learned that the only prayer needed is for the unknown good for individuals or situations - beyond this to *do* nothing unless a series of coincidences and events occur which make such action very clear.

I am interested in the great Ocean of Silence. What do we understand its nature to be? What has Science to teach us? I believe there are Angels and beings who care for us. I think that they come around us when we really need them and can go away when we are negative. Exactly what or who God is I am not sure: Love, of course, but I do not think of a Person but a Supreme Being in Whom and through Whom All Is One!

U.F.O.s

A religious experience is a very high speed experience which cannot be completely remembered or described in words.

I saw my first U.F.O. in the autumn of 1989. Being technically-minded and knowing much about U.F.O.s and our things in the sky, I am convinced it was not one of ours.

I think this work is important. Please consider way-out ideas. There is a vast field of new knowledge opening up.

ANSWERS TO PRAYERS

In my own life I think there have been two different kinds of spiritual experience: answers to prayers, which have changed my life, and unexplained visions or feelings which I can remember well but which did not have any lasting effect.

'TURN IN, TURN IN'

One reason why the spoken word transcends the written word is that it can speak only to the *Now*, when it is uttered. As we live and die daily, we change, and the answer to the question changes.

Now, this writer says that every experience is 'religious'. From the moment we begin to develop an ego (and more and more egos) the entire life of anyone who is a Seeker after Truth is a re-search for the Oneness which we truly are. It is a research for our own immortality, for the 'that of God' in us, that we may have ceased to *BE*, since 'the shades of the prison-house begin to close upon the growing boy'. The child's natural *feel* becomes swamped by the world's over-think, but deep in every heart there are intimations - more, confirmations - of our immortality which, if we do not stop-up our inner ears, will whisper eternally 'Turn in, turn in!' and warn us of seeking (as Othello did) 'the ocular proof'.

Quaker worship concentrates the love of two or three (or more) gathered together and speaks to contemplatives individually or through the spoken word, which transcends the letter of almost all other ways of worship. It is essentially an experience of the Timeless Ever-Present Presence, which is Now, whether in or outside Meeting. This is religious experience.

WELT-SCHMERZ

I certainly prefer to use the word 'spiritual' to 'religious'; it seems more accurately to describe the place where the experiences come from. 'Religious' has all sorts of other connotations about sanctity, sacrament, institutions etc.

The word 'otherness' seems more comfortable to me than 'God' - at least, sometimes it does and certainly in relation to spiritual experiences. Occasionally I could firmly ascribe the experiences to something called God. But often it is much more nebulous than that.

To me, religious experience is a sense of 'otherness' which cannot be described in any other way: a sense of the presence of God/power/totality/wholeness - sometimes within myself (immanent), at other times from outside myself (transcendent).

It may manifest itself as this feeling of intense awareness (sometimes it is a self-awareness). It may be a sudden clear answer to a problem, a dilemma, or a cry for help. It feels like a parting of clouds, an incredible lightness of being. It is often followed by a sensation of great joy and assurance and strength, a certainty that all is well. But sometimes it is followed by a surge of 'welt-schmerz', a sudden consciousness of suffering humanity, identification with the pain of the world - as though *I* was God - or Jesus.

Triggers to spiritual experience exist everywhere, anywhere, but not so often (for me) in the expected areas like art, music or the natural world.

GOD-GUIDED

Until recently I think I limited religious experience, in my mind, to that of the ancient prophets, for example, Isaiah in the Temple (*Is.6*) or to St Paul on the road to Damascus. That is to say, to what may be termed a transcendent or unusual or even an abnormal experience. As I have myself never had such an experience I cannot report or describe it.

My wife died some three and a half years ago. It was a shattering blow to me. It affected my general feelings and attitude. I have come round to the following view.

There would seem to be three types of religious experience: the transcendent (this would seem to be an abnormal or unusual experience and to be divided into two forms). First, a form when voices and visions are experienced in the mind, as vivid auditory images and vivid visual images: in non-technical language, as vivid imagination, but God-guided. Some of the prophetic sayings may come into this category.

Then there is the form when voices and visions seem to be external, quite outside the person experiencing them. Finally, there is the ordinary, common or garden experience of God. We tend to take it for granted and do not trouble to investigate it.

SPIRITUAL HUG

In my own life I understand spiritual experience to mean the moments of sudden enlightenment, of emotional response, of heightened awareness that seem to stand outside time. They can occur in the most unlikely setting as well as during times of planned recollection. In colloquial terms my own definition would be that they are a sort of spiritual hug ! They can cause us to cry out, to smile or laugh out loud, or to cry, just as when something tender is said to us by someone we love.

MANIFESTATIONS OF HIS SPIRIT

Religious experience is to me the times when one is in direct contact with God, and feels the manifestations of His spirit. This happens so frequently (especially when one is 'in extremis') as to be a commonplace.

DEATHS ... LEAD TO LIFE ?

Anything 'special' has been rare in my life. God is, and must remain, a mystery, but God is everywhere and in all things: in all events, all relationships, all experiences.

In a sense, I feel that spiritual experience is at its most vital when it is an experience of death. The little (and not so little) deaths through which, painfully and painstakingly, we have to thread our way can, perhaps most of all, lead to life ? This has been very much *my* spiritual experience.

ANYTHING NEWLY-BORN

Spiritual experiences seem to happen to me when one or more of several conditions is being experienced. Such as when I feel part of and at one with the whole of God's creation; when I am involved in a traumatic situation and I can only pray for guidance; when I am totally absorbed by the creativity and wonder of others through music, a painting, words and anything newly born; when I am meditating and my mind is free of wandering thoughts and in a state of relaxed awareness, a special kind of prepared readiness.

The common factors seem to be a stillness and a silence into which words (not a voice) come with a very special feeling of being at peace, of being surrounded by God's love, and of just 'knowing', that is being given a special and essential truth. In the best possible sense I am and I know. It only lasts a very short while, but it is a very clear, gentle but firm sensation that leaves a calmness, peace and joy. Nothing, it seems, can take away the experience or the 'afterglow'. Both remain with me for a long time. I can return to them quite easily when I recall the particular circumstances.

Drop Deeply Within Myself

In my understanding, God is silence, the void, the uncreated, the background of the picture whose foreground is the world of humanity - no image does more than suggest a direction.

Twenty years or so of worshipping 'after the manner of Friends' have taught me that there are routes which I can attempt to take; that these attempts to make contact are a deeply meaningful exercise; and that, having opened channels up, something sometimes comes back along them - sometimes when I am not trying - and takes me by surprise. I think this element of surprise must be one of my criteria. It suggests that I have struck something 'other'. If I sit silently and drop deeply within myself, my words eventually crumble into silence, my thoughts trail off, my images disintegrate.

Although what happens after this is ineffable, after a while the silence seeds new thoughts, images and words. As I haul the experience up toward the light of common day, it takes increasing shape. For one thing, it shapes itself like the experience of communication with another person; this is because *I* am a person and only have the patterning for relating to other persons. For another, the form takes on the particular shape of *my* temperament, *my* mental resources, *my* vocabulary so that the final form is both essentially me, and yet not me. At the core of the experience is something I do not feel I could have produced on my own, or in any other way: I accept it as something 'given' and treat it with reverence.

It is like a child absorbed in the contemplation of what to an adult are just a few common sea shells. For me, the experiences continue to yield joy and peace and meaning. They carry a conviction that authenticates them though for another they might seem trivial. I think this is because the experiences only have meaning in their context in my life, while they are like signposts, sometimes indicating a turning-point.

A POWERFULLY-SENSED AWARENESS
I would define a religious/spiritual experience as a powerfully-sensed awareness of another dimension to normal, everyday life which adds a sense of illumination/insight/meaning/purpose/conviction/holiness to an otherwise conventional experience.

IRRADIATED BY TOTAL LOVE
The meaning of religious or spiritual experience is to me a spontaneous but essentially uplifting 'happening' that cannot be explained in scientific or material terms. From my own personal experience, it is like suddenly being surrounded and irradiated by total love - like coming into brilliant sunshine out of the dark - a condition of being where there is no more fear and quite literally a peace that 'passes all understanding'.

In the peace and quiet of a gathered Meeting for Worship I feel we are 'tuning in' to this total love, and the inner light this inspires can lead to ministry that is helpful and meaningful to all.

THE SENSE OF GIFT

What I take to be religious experience has six qualities: truth, givenness, certainty about the truth, unexpectedness of the experience, an association with positive emotional feeling and an impact which lasts for months or years.

I understand these truths to be different from scientific discoveries, and as being 'given' and made available to me through that of God in me. As well as the sense of Gift I have felt a certainty, there was no need to question or doubt, quite simply I 'knew' the truth and meaning of what was given.

I do not believe that these experiences are a form of psychological denial or defence which might leave the subject stronger or comforted in a blind way. They seem to lead to an increase in mature resilience. They *feel* different from dreams/imagination/fantasy and even many meditative states or prayer. In my experience they cannot be planned or induced - though the memory of an experience may be imbued with some of the same emotions it is clearly a memory, and not the experience.

EXISTENCE IS A SPIRITUAL ACHIEVEMENT

Everything outward, objective, public to do with our concern for God and the sacred, I call religion. That which is inward, subjective, personal, I see as spiritual. That which is inward creates that which is outward. Existence is a spiritual achievement.

BEING PART OF A WHOLE

In any marriage, especially with a family, there is (in addition to all the temporal considerations) a spiritual side which informs the tenderest feelings which bind together (whether realised or not) in a religious experience to realise the oneness of the world and the whole cosmos under a protecting spirit of love which is 'God'.

When I consider what we call life I am always overwhelmed with feelings of wonder, of the privilege of being part of a whole. A raising of the spirit to a worshipping height, with the mystery of the very fact of life - a part of spirit.

The discovery of the interconnectedness of all life; that it is a whole; that the spiritual side is integral with all else; that it is all a glorious adventure (not only personally but including all generations) to enjoy together with all life on mother earth: this is what I would think of as spiritual experience and what could be termed religious in that God or Love is its basis.

This thought of spirit being the most real and taking precedence over the material and temporal, becomes a source of comfort and hope, realising this spirit of love without limit throughout the universe, yet immanent in our lives - this makes worship so much more natural.

ALL IS VIBRATING

My spiritual experience is an on-going thing - an uplifting feeling of things of nature, and that sense of Oneness with people, with animals and with nature; where all is vibrating and contributing to a wholeness of Creation.

COMMENT

These replies (to the question repeated at the start) tell us what each contributor understands by this type of experience. They were not asked for a general opinion, based on reading, theory or doctrine, and where these were described I have excluded them. This may seem high-handed but it is important to keep to the actual question and the basis of the whole enquiry. This is the actual experience of individuals who are writing at first-hand.

These replies form a mosaic of what these men and women understand by the terms religious (or spiritual) experience from what has actually happened to them, which they will describe when answering the second query.

Mosaic is an apt word in its figurative dictionary meaning, 'a diversified whole' (*Concise Oxford*). Because there is no precise language for these subjective experiences it is not at first easy to see the whole from the pieces that compose it. I have made this attempt by entering on cards the main descriptive words used in the replies and then sorting them as one does in making an index. They fall into six convenient categories, as follow:

General characteristics - mainly non-personal
The experiences are valuable and important to the individual. They are intense and of lasting influence. They come unbidden, as a surprise. They signify the reality of spirit, a special dimension of experience that is something different from normal day-to-day reality. They are evidence of 'something other' or 'something else', a specific realm of consciousness, beyond intellect.

Such an experience is characterised by feeling or mood. It is a form of contact, communication or communion of a superior quality - an illumination or perception that makes a turning-point or signpost. It consists of intimations or confirmations that may change one's life. These experiences are normally good and testify to the unity and interconnectedness of life. They promote the spiritual growth and wisdom of the individual.

General characteristics - mainly personal
The experience affects the whole self. It induces a heightened awareness through insight and intuition, like seeing new light. Essentially it is a vivid awareness that carries conviction and yields change, promotes healing and provides controlled and purposive power for change and creativity.

Positive Influences
Such experiences are characterised by joy and comfort, a calm wonder and a feeling of peace, by love and gentleness, tenderness, hope and caring. For the individual, they are meaningful and transforming.

Negative Influences
Some have no lasting effect and are forgotten. They may produce an identification with pain and suffering or a negative set-back in personal growth through guilt or despair.

Reference to God
These are experiences of mystery and they induce reverence. They are evidence of contact with God and God's love in his creation. They signify 'that of God' or of love in the world and provide a relationship that is timeless yet always and everywhere present. In this event God may be regarded as Spirit, the Supreme Being, 'Otherness', a Higher Power or as Jesus.

Techniques

Religious or spiritual experiences may be sought through different means, sources and conditions. A deliberate technique may be used. A prepared readiness in silence and stillness or an attitude of worship is helpful. Prayer, meditation and attendance at Meeting for Worship are appropriate. Nature provides a source, through nature mysticism. Other sources are a God-guided imagination, visions or voices, words, anything new-born, music, painting, dreams and an awareness of angels or spirits.

PART II

EXPERIENCES

Replies to Second Question

(Note: The sequence of replies is not the same as in *Part I*)

Can you describe a religious (or spiritual) experience that has happened to yourself ?

I AM PART OF THE LAUGHTER

About ten years ago I attended Meeting for Worship. I was asking the question 'Now that my daughters are growing up, how am I to spend the rest of my life?' I was asking, and asking very seriously, for guidance about vocation, hoping for light on retraining for a second career. As there was no sign of an answer I prodded the subject in a rather desultory way.

Suddenly I began to feel that there *was* an answer, and that I was moving towards it. I can't remember my thoughts, just an almost physical sense of anticipation. Then I knew that I was almost there - I only had to reach out; I did so eagerly and found my mind full of a very trite pop-song that I must have picked up from my daughter's transistor during the week: 'It ain't what you do, it's the way that you do it'.

I didn't know how to react; I felt let down, amused, irritated, confused; if it had to be music, why not something more majestic, or why not a newer, more socially-significant song? The rational part of me said, 'There, that is what you get for being silly; of course God doesn't answer questions like that'. The less rational part kept this memory clear when much else from the period faded into new preoccupations.

Two years ago I found myself back at the same Meeting and the memory, with something of the anticipation, returned. I think I must have turned it over occasionally in the intervening period. In reflecting, I found that it *was* the answer, but a much more profound answer than I had been looking for.

It made me take responsibility for my own life-choices, opened me to the unexpected and unorthodox in a way I have found quite challenging, and forced me to seek the leading of the spirit in the everyday details of whatever life I was leading. If the question wasn't *What?* then it must be *How?* and so *Why?*. It takes me a lot further than I had any thought of going when I posed the question. When I refer back to it I find that I grin, sometimes happily, sometimes rather grimly; it *was* funny, and the joke was on me, yet I am part of the laughter, too.

My husband and I were driving through country lanes in Normandy. He was at the wheel and I was idly looking at the view. It wasn't anything remarkable. As we drove along, I suddenly glimpsed a field gateway overgrown with wild flowers and grasses; the next vehicle to use the gate would have flattened them. With this glimpse came the words 'seeing with the eyes of God'.

I felt that I had seen something ordinary and ephemeral in all its beauty, had seen creation as God sees it. When the visual memory returns (which it does spontaneously) it reminds me that I need to pay more attention to the way in which I look at things; I begin to wonder, Does God try to teach us to look at people and situations in His way, or is it that God in some way needs *our* looking, needs us to be his eyes as well as his hands?

The original feelings of wonder and awe continued throughout the afternoon as we explored the spectacular cliffs and sat watching patterns of sunlight and shadow race over the textured surface of the sea. Yet I know that the previous experience was the important one.

AN INSTRUMENT OF PERCEPTION

The most vivid and important moment in my life was one which went beyond the normal bounds of perception. It took place a few years ago and would, I suppose, be described as a 'peak experience', but how clinical and pseudo-scientific that makes it sound! It was - unusually, I think, for such experiences - shared with another person.

We had just been through a time of great difficulty and had reached a very painful decision. As we parted, we were each enveloped by what seemed a cloak descending about us. The feeling was utterly benign, and quite unlike anything I had ever felt before, or have felt since. We did not discuss what had happened at the time, apart from acknowledging it, but later wrote about it independently of one another in almost identical terms.

I now realise that those few moments - lasting perhaps half a minute - were the most important in my life, and are something to which I can return, if only as a less intense recollection, in times of doubt and difficulty. I mention this deeply precious moment with some diffidence, as it can so easily smack of spiritual pride. I do so, however, because I know such experiences are in fact quite widespread, and because I have always drawn such comfort from the accounts others have given of similar experiences. Indeed, such personal testimony has always seemed much more valuable to me than fine-spun intellectual argument.

I know that this experience had nothing to do with my apparent individual 'self' or ego. That sense is very strong, and means that pride simply does not come into it; instead there is a sense of deep privilege. This in turn has the effect of lifting an enormous burden, and is deeply comforting.

A second experience has also been very important to me. It occurred in the course of a 'polarity' therapy session, in which I had got in touch with a particular part of myself that can be a source of considerable trouble, namely the 'Rescuer'.

At a certain point something snapped and I simply became aware of the therapist talking away in the background. I knew vaguely that he was delivering a lecture to the Rescuer but I was no longer listening to the words. It was as though the normal conscious mind had short-circuited. The most amazing, faraway sensation crept over me, in which I felt I was floating and at once extraordinarily light and extraordinarily heavy. I was all but incapable of speech.

None of the normal presenters of my personality were any longer in place; it was a state of just being, of awareness, of being swept along. It was an experience permeated by bliss, lasting I suppose about ten minutes. Again it was unlike anything I had felt before, and in the virtual loss of self I felt there was some deep spiritual contact or significance.

Whatever it was I felt, it had nothing to do with the apparent, everyday me and the construct of my personality, but had a universal quality about it. It was, I would think, very close to what is called 'pure consciousness', in which the 'self' is reduced to no more than an observer, who returns to tell the tale.

Quite frequently in meditation, moments come as I let go and get swept up in some Greater Whole when I feel poised on the brink of an abyss. I find myself checking myself at the last moment, rather than throwing myself off into some abyss where I would no longer have control, and from which I might never return - or so it feels.

I have often wondered what this moment of slipping in and then jerking back means. What is the abyss, and why am I afraid of abandoning myself to it? Is it just fear of losing my self-identity?

One morning in Meeting a number of such 'waves' came over me, with such force that at times I thought, 'If I go with one of these waves - if I step off the edge of the abyss - the impact will be so strong that I will cry out aloud or make some sort of scene'. But perhaps the reassurance of the group helped me to go further than ever before.

The waves came as I allowed myself to be flooded by the wonder of my life at that time, so rich and full - although certainly not without difficulties. To be alive, I felt, was an immense joy and privilege. I saw myself as an instrument of perception, taking in the world around me, and able, in a way that was quite overwhelming when I thought of it, to discern the divine in so much of life. All I could do was to bring that joy back to the source from which it had come.

And then, as in a flash, it came to me: the Source and Perception are one. The miracle that I, a sentient being, could perceive the greater whole was grounded in the Source itself. The Source was, somehow, mirroring itself, or extending itself, through the agency of perception. The enigmatic, profound Hindu words 'That thou art', or 'Thou art That', came to mind. The separateness was illusory; in the act of perceiving we were inextricably bound up with the fount and origin of all that was.

THE FEATURES OF CHRIST

Two different spiritual experiences were vivid enough to be remembered after thirty years. The first happened when I was becoming interested in Quakerism. I was attending evening classes, and the tutor often impressed me by his patience and warm response to a very loquacious student.

On one such occasion when the student was being particularly difficult, I saw the tutor's face change and to my surprise - I recognised the features of Christ - just for a fleeting moment. I somehow knew that my recognition came from a deep memory, not from any religious painting I had ever seen. For me this was authentic and I didn't doubt my 'vision' for a moment. Incidentally, I later discovered that the tutor was a Friend!

Another experience was when I was climbing a cliff, all alone, leaving the family below in the care of my sister. I felt detached and delightfully free, then came a feeling of weight-lessness, of expanding into the sky and sea. This I recognised as an experience of leaving my physical body and being born into a spiritual dimension - for a fleeting moment. 'Coming down to earth' is a descriptive phrase! I had taken up a new career in housing management which I found really fulfilling but sometimes difficult and exhausting. I always dreaded Monday mornings when there were so many problems to deal with after weekends of family rows, leaking roofs etc.

One Monday I just said 'Oh God, if there is a God, please help me to deal wisely with the tenants this morning' and promptly forgot about it. However while having my lunch I suddenly remembered how smoothly the morning had gone and was convinced it was the answer to prayer and that there must be a God. But I was also rather frightened because I realised life could not really be as easy as that, and this experience inhibited me from praying again for a long while. Even now I am very careful in what I pray about - 'God is a Spirit and should be worshipped in Spirit'.

Some time after this I got to know about the Religious Society of Friends and eventually became a member. One Sunday in Meeting for Worship the ministry included the sentence 'A child who has not received much love finds it very difficult to give love as an adult' and immediately I recognised that this was what was wrong with me. I started praying often to be made more loving and at a residential Yearly Meeting that year the prayer 'Make me an instru-ment of Thy peace and reconciliation' kept on running through my head. A few weeks later I was guided into being just that.

HAVING WALKED ON THE WATER

The Church, of which I was an active member, was served by a rota of ordained ministers and local preachers. At one particular evening service, when I was in my early twenties, I settled down to twenty minutes of boring sermon by one of the least inspiring local preachers. His technique was to take a biblical text and systematically flog it to death.

I can't remember what text he took that evening, except that it was something to do with 'light'. What I recall vividly is that everything he said was, literally, 'illuminated' with deep meaning. Every phrase, every word, seemed to penetrate my mind as statements of absolute truth.

I don't think, objectively, he was any different from his normal performance. My reaction was quite different from thinking 'He's good for a change'. The whole experience of listening (absorbing would be a better word) was unaccountably transformed.

It was a transient experience: the only lasting effect was to invest the word 'light' with new significance - and this was long before I had come across the Society of Friends.

I had attended a day conference on the message of George Fox and was singularly unimpressed. One of the other participants was staying with me overnight and I made my feelings very plain to him. We discussed the theme of the day until late that evening and resumed at breakfast next morning. I made no bones about my distaste for the evangelical approach to religion.

My dissatisfaction stayed with me for the remainder of the second day and I had a restless night. I was nagged by the feeling that I was putting up internal barriers to the love of God. I wanted the 'hound of heaven' to go away! Eventually, exhausted and confused, I sank to my knees in the security of the bathroom and prayed something brief like 'not my will, but thine', without reservation.

The effect was immediate and unexpected. I felt the presence of a Christ-like person by my side (metaphorically, not literally) but 'he' was quite different from what I might have expected. Much more like a reassuring, helpful, non-judgmental brother or friend.

The awareness of this presence continued for over two months and had a positive effect on my behaviour, I think (I didn't dare mention any of this to anyone). The truth of religion as a relationship, not a system of belief and morality, was borne in on me as a reality.

My reaction to religious writing was also transformed. Previously, I had a positive aversion to reading the Bible. Now the *New Testament* - particularly the *Acts of the Apostles* - came alive; it was almost as though the words were illuminated on the page and George Fox's words about reading the scriptures in the light of the Spirit became a reality. I found Fox's epistles full of meaning for the first time. And the most surprising change was my reaction to the writings of Thomas R. Kelly.

I had been given one of his books, *The Eternal Promise*, some years before but found his writing excessively flowery and emotional; like wading through sickly treacle. But when I read it again, it seemed an almost prosaic, factual manual of religious experience. One thing which was not transformed by my new state of mind was Meeting for Worship, much to my disappointment.

This 'state of mind' finished as abruptly as it began. It was almost as though, having 'walked on the water' for ten weeks, I looked down, lost my nerve and sank down to my earlier rather sceptical frame of mind.

Was it 'real' or self-induced illusion? I don't know. I think it has left me with a deeper understanding of the very personal, evangelical brand of religion and the sneaking feeling that it is for real but I haven't got the courage to accept it !

ORIGINAL INSPIRATION

My limited experience does not include anything remotely dramatic. Nor can I associate with it anything which could be taken as an indication of a personality. Perhaps such a concept is for us earthbound spirits only. I have grouped my experiences into five types. If these have any significance, I am not aware of it.

a. Sudden, inexplicable moments of joy and longer, unexplained moments of depression.

The joy is a feeling of love/excitement/interest/anticipation. It last seconds but is remembered. It is not correlated particularly with life going well. The depression is a feeling of uselessness/pain/boredom/guilt. It lasts minutes and may re-occur at times over days. Such moments are experienced about a few times a year.

b. Inspiration and creativity.

'Good' ideas in one's fields of interest (in my case physics and art). These come in seconds out of the blue but always require very hard work to realise. The ideas persist for a while in the memory but then fade away. Quite often there is an interaction between the original inspiration and its subsequent realisation. Sometimes the original inspiration is not understood until it is part realised. Painting a picture is a good example of this.

c. Reality and the 'real' world.

On a few occasions in my life I have experienced a sudden and completely unexpected feeling lasting a minute or so where all sense of the 'here and now' is lost. A 'What am I doing here?' sort of feeling. There is also a feeling of panic - will I be able to get back into my normal life? It was especially disturbing when this happened in company.

More predictably, I am always completely convinced of the nebulous nature of our physical world when regarding consciousness after an anaesthetic.

d. Supernormal communication.

The whole phenomena of the empathy and unspoken under-standing which can exist between individuals and groups goes well beyond any scientific understanding of the different ways with which we can communicate. I recall one particular occasion with a group of students of several nationalities where a deep discussion was in progress in spite of the fact that nobody understood the languages of the others in the group. It is also evident that in many meetings for worship held by Friends there is a considerable communica-tion in silence in the meeting. This is not a phenomenon you could 'prove'. It is one you would 'know' if you were there.

e. Response to appeals for help.

At times in my life when I have been stretched physically, mentally or emotionally, to what I thought was my limit and have prayed for help (unspecified - I did not know what to ask for) then unlikely but ordinary things happened and my problems faded away.

THE MYSTIC ROSE

I can recall having had three 'peak' experiences of a quasi-mystical kind during my life, though I believe only one of them can properly be classified as religious, the other two being more in the nature of aesthetic experiences. I find it hard to make appropriate distinctions in this area.

The religious experience occurred at a time of acute mental conflict when I was undergoing a severe identity crisis.

I had a remarkable dream one Sunday night, such as I had never had before. I dreamt that through a partly opened door, behind which shone a strange, ineffable light, I caught a glimpse of a red rose of supreme unearthly beauty.

'It's the mystic rose !' I exclaimed to myself in my dream, and for what seemed several seconds, during which I was lost in awe and wonderment, I had an intense feeling of indescribable happiness.

Finding on awakening that I had no clear idea what the phrase 'the mystic rose' meant, I did some research at the local library, where I discovered that 'the rose was a symbol of spiritual revelation, the reward of the pilgrim at the end of his search' and that it represented 'the flower of the spirit attainable to man through sacrifice'.

The feeling that I had received some sort of visitation persisted throughout the whole of the following week and culminated on September 15th in the conviction that I was called upon to found a new Order of Charity, whose form instantaneously presented itself to my mind.

Called the Society of St James, the Order would have as its motto 'Faith through Works' (after Chapter 1, verse 27 of the *General Epistle of James*). It would consist of lay men and women taking a vow and living under a rule. They could be of any religious denomination or none, but must believe in the Universe's underlying spiritual basis.

Members of the Society (called Jamesians) would be pledged to a threefold charity: that of bringing hope to the young, courage to the sick and comfort to the old. But it would be a charitable association unlike any other. Jamesians would seek to form an intimate personal relationship with someone in each of the above-mentioned categories. Their aim would be to make the lonely persons of their adoption feel that they belonged to someone, that they counted as persons and that their lives mattered.

Though mildly awestruck at what had happened to me, my first reaction was that I should carry on with my normal life until my vocation was somehow confirmed. Over the next four to five years I embarked at intervals on a number of sporadic initiatives to test my fitness for my mission - more from a sense of duty, I believe, than anything else, because my enthusiasm was slowly waning and my doubts about it increasing more and more.

Though my dream had been an unexpected and inexplicable event, it had not yet proved powerful enough to make me seriously want to change my way of life.

Mary Who was Crying over Me

The first time I had anything like this was when I was twenty-five and not at all a religious person. I had an operation after an ectopic pregnancy and I had a 'near death' experience.

I was not clear at all what had happened to me but when I talked about it to the hospital chaplain and told him that I had gone through a tunnel into the most beautiful place with colours and sounds like I had never known and then been pulled back into a fearful place I did not want to go into, he explained more sympathetically that he had known others have this same experience.

A couple of years ago my son was seriously ill and I had several amazing experiences. Some are not easy to describe. On one occasion I was sitting at home and seemed to be surrounded (the only way I can describe it) by Jesus who was comforting me but also bleeding over me and Mary who was crying over me. It sounds awful but was incredibly beautiful.

Another time I saw Christ in the sunlight in my garden. I also had a vision of my son being carried by the twelve apostles and then I was with him in hospital and I saw people sitting having picnics and a voice said it was 'the final peace'. I have been able to channel (I think it is called) since then, that is I write messages, only it is not me, I am just the person that the writing is done through. I don't do this very often because I don't want to abuse this mystical power. Here is one such message which I received when my son was ill.

My dear Carol
Your love is carrying you forward. How blessed is your life, and the hunger and thirst ceasing. When the clocks finish their time and the clothing of the world's weariness is over, then

will we celebrate the joy that has been won. Wonder and love and tenderness come together so that the sighing ceases. You have heard with your hands together. Let them embrace your friends and loved ones and touch the limits of the Lord's prayings. How soon comes the end of despair and despondency. And love reigns. Hasten to the good time and know that the wells are full.

AROMA OF HOME-MADE BISCUITS

While on a bird-watching holiday one member of the party and myself decided that we had walked far enough so we sat down at the path's edge above a steep ravine. We talked for a few minutes then lapsed into silence, contemplating the view and resting after a fairly strenuous morning. To my surprise (yet it did not seem to be unusual) the small reddish-brown head of a weasel appeared over the rim of the ravine. Its shiny black eyes took in the landscape and the two resting humans, as if all was normal. As its eyes met mine we were as one in a world where all are interdependent and yet all are individuals; all are equal and of equal worth.

I felt full of joy and very privileged to have seen this lovely creature in its own environment, unafraid and active and I felt a response towards it as another creature on this earth. The whole episode was over in seconds, I suppose, but its effect still seems to cover a life-time of relationships.

After asking Meeting for Worship for prayers to be said and support and love to be given to a couple whose daughter had just died, I sat down and I was not unduly surprised by the almost overwhelming sense of loving support and the presence of God which filled the room. To my surprise I became aware of another presence in meeting. Always when I am aware of this happening I need to ask within myself who it is; somehow I know instinctively when the answer is correct. Clearly some answers will be obvious, as in this case, as it was the daughter who wished to convey a message to her parents and family. There was also a delicious aroma of home-made biscuits, I could see the shape of the biscuits and the shape of a special small tree. The parents and I were often in contact both before and after the sad event.

Our daughter had to have a suspicious 'lump' removed and I prayed that it would prove to be benign. At a very low ebb in my prayers I could not think of what to say, all words seemed inappropriate and useless. In the silence of despair words seemed to be there telling me to ask that the right answer for our daughter be given to her. I knew then that my prayer had to be worded in that way because whatever the answer might be we would be given the necessary strength to deal with the events in the future.

THE EVERLASTING HILLS

When I was sixteen I went, with my parents, to stay with an uncle and aunt in their stone farmhouse. It was in high Pennine country, which was new to me. On the face of it, this was not likely to be a significant life-experience. However I have in fact long regarded its impact as seminal.

The whole ethos and rhythm of their life-style was different from ours, which was distinctly suburban. But the great impact for me lay in the setting, in the backdrop to it all. Time and again I sat in a deep window-seat, looking down the field and across the valley to the 'everlasting hills' (as I called them) on the far side.

The whole experience bit deep into my consciousness. It introduced me, at a conscious level, to the eternal in the contemporary. I have to describe it as spiritual (or religious). My horizons were so gloriously widened that when, some five years later, I was introduced to writers in the Western contemplative tradition, I knew that they spoke to me.

And now, half a century later, I recognize that the seeds of a lifelong spirituality, no doubt dormant in the unconscious, began to germinate in that experience among the northern hills.

God's Love Mediated

I was walking to hospital for a cancer operation when about half-way there (I can remember exactly where this took place) I had a strong feeling of being enfolded in love and a wonderful calm which stayed with me throughout my stay in hospital and recovery at home. This was felt both as a direct relationship with a loving God and also as God's love mediated through the hospital personnel and my friends and family.

By His Proximity

My first religious experience was twenty-eight years ago. I was a single parent with three children. The youngest was four. She was in hospital with torticollis and was on the danger list, though I did not realise this. I was distraught and exhausted with trying to cope with thrice-daily visits to the hospital on my bicycle, and with the normal care of the nine and seven year olds.

One night I thumped violently on my pillow and said 'God, I don't believe you, but you've got to be there, because I need your help!' I fell asleep quite calmly and in the morning was aware of renewed strength. Local Friends helped in various ways (I was new to the area), my daughter finally recovered and my life returned to normal. But of course I was now aware of God's existence and have since found that He is always there for me when I pray to Him. In fact, I can measure the extent of my difficulties by His proximity.

An Eternal Fountain

In early adult life when I was twenty-seven, I had to leave England with my husband and daughter to go overseas. I had missed many Springs through study and urban living. I decided to make a last pilgrimage to the bluebell woods but, to my disappointment, the experience failed me. There was joy, but no extension of consciousness.

However when we reached our destination, for the first time I had a clear vision of God. Although I was the passive recipient of this experience, the accompanying circumstance was illuminating.

My husband, quite unjustifiably, lost his temper with our African house-boy, who was doing nothing whatever wrong. It was the spontaneous Christian reaction of the house-boy (who kept his dignity, but nonetheless by his calmness and gentleness turned away my husband's wrath) which suddenly vividly illustrated for me the whole meaning of the

Sermon on the Mount and the teaching of Jesus. This seemed to tear away a veil in my heart and I saw the light of God shining down on us like a sun and an eternal fountain, whose beams or rays were all light, life and love. It penetrated and illuminated my heart, like a spiritual chamber, and caused me to pour forth love in return.

I must emphasise that this was a *spiritual* beholding, and not a physical or mental 'seeing'. From then on I knew that I was spirit as well as mind and body. I then understood that although my childhood experiences had been an opening into the ambience of God, the dynamic and luminous source had at those times remained hidden.

This has also illustrated for me the different experiences which lead people to conclude 'pantheism' or 'God immanent' or 'God transcendent'. All are true within limitations. It is a wonderful revelation to receive all these beholdings at one time, and to find the limitations of personal consciousness melting away so that one need no longer feel any distinction between 'inward' and 'outward'.

The wonderful revelation I had in our first months remained an enormous source of strength and inspiration, and did recur. The most vivid return of the vision was when walking along beside a beautiful river, when the vision remained throughout the walk: between forty minutes and an hour, I think. As I returned to the car I made the resolution that I would hold on to this vision and carry it with me. Immediately that the thoughts entered my mind, the experience was withdrawn! 'I' of course can do nothing, these things are given, and are not for us to determine.

Another outcome of the experience has been belief in spiritual healing. For some time after I first found God I was still troubled by the knowledge of so much pain and suffering, mostly undeserved and seemingly striking in a random way. Then one day it came to me that this was what the teaching of the Kingdom was all about. The Good News was that the Kingdom was already potentially present. We were called to come under the government of Love, and once this was fully accepted and commanded whole-hearted belief, then sickness and suffering would vanish away.

A Tree of Cascading Blossoms

In a period of prayer and meditation I had been besieging the heavens with demands to know what to *do* with the gifts I have. The image that came was of a tree in flower - all the delicate, glorious beauty of a blossoming tree - but so easily buffeted by wind and rain. The task seemed to nurture and tend this tree to bring it to the stage where it could bear its fruit.

Suddenly I saw the relevance of a dream I had almost eleven years ago - soon after one of my closest friends, sister-close, had committed suicide. It was so real it seemed no dream at all. Again I had been besieging the heavens for explanations - demands to know where she was. In the dream Anna came back, sat beside me, held my hand, reassured. All was truly well with her. I was the one who tried to cling, to no avail.

After she had gone, I found myself standing under a tree of cascading blossoms, white flowers - and can feel the ecstasy still of that beauty. I tried to pick a flower, from the left - to take back to Robert, but it melted in my hand like snow. I managed to pick one from a branch on my right, put it in my bag and set out to find my way home to Robert. The rest of the dream was about that long journey, never completed, which became more arduous, the landscape increasingly drear as I struggled upwards and back.

Before this morning's image came I had suspicions that part at least of my task was to bring beauty to the world in some way, in art, writing, daily doings, whatever. That sounds wildly pompous - but I see it more as an orientation rather than a 'mission'. The painting, the writing, the laughter are all aspects of the same beauty - religious experience.

As an undergraduate I was in an essay crisis - writing into the small hours to get it finished before the next day's tutorial. I was struggling with a German poet, an ode to an Aeolian harp. It was about memories of a dead child, his brother, echoes of memory like wind sounding the strings of an Aeolian harp. I re-read and re-read, trying to concentrate the meaning out of the poem. Something dissolved in me, and everything was clear - the poem, everything, life simply. An ecstatic sense of relief and joy and certainty and knowing. I didn't tell anyone, but carried the wonder of it like a secret, for a long time.

I'd been a very 'religious' person but at that stage was fast losing any faith I'd had. This experience was *real* in comparison to everything that went before, or indeed since, and started me off on a long questing road.

THE GREATNESS OF THE CREATOR

On more than one occasion, when walking in woodlands and absorbing the sights, sounds, smells, and the general air of peace and timelessness, I have been acutely aware of the Spirit, the Creator. It has been far more than an enjoyable out-of-door relaxation. It has been transforming - and that is a key word.

Similarly, when standing on a bracing clifftop or rocky shore, facing an angry sea, I have felt the nearness and the greatness of the Creator. And in mountains.

Once, on a terribly gloomy November day when I was thoroughly depressed, a kingfisher emerged from the drainpipe under my feet (I was crossing a dyke at the time) and darted off at incredible speed. He was far more than a bright, swift bird. He, too, was a transforming experience. It can happen in buildings, too, though not elaborate, grand, stately ones. A tiny, shabby, humble chapel, which looks more like a cow-byre, is very special to me. I make a point of going there whenever I go to the West Country, and the Spirit is quite definitely in that building. Incidentally, one can leave requests for prayers there. I have done so, and have had quite miraculous answers to those prayers.

The same sense of the presence of the Spirit has been strongly there in other ancient places but, for me, one essential element is simplicity of surroundings. Pomp and wealth seem to be an enormous barrier.

In contrast to the foregoing place-related experiences, I share with a huge number of other people a sense of wonder and marvel of life whenever I see a new baby or a young animal. This never fails and, in presence of such new life, I know that I am in the presence of the Creator of all life.

Very rarely, a 'gathered' Quaker Meeting is a truly spiritual experience. It happens to me roughly once a year.

SURGE OF INTENSE JOY

It was a dull, wet day, my mind was occupied with the class I was going to teach, and I was running rather late. I drove along a familiar and unremarkable stretch of road and was obliged to slow down for a tractor. I looked out of my car window and saw a black and white cat stalking quietly through the long wet grass of a nearby garden. For no definable reason, I felt a sudden surge of intense joy. I was reminded of the futility of worrying about being late, about the history class. I was touched by the grace and easy solitariness of the cat. It was only a moment or two before the cat disappeared, the tractor trundled down a side lane and I drove on, but the feeling of joy stayed with me for the whole day and I still recall it with great pleasure.

Was that a spiritual experience? The same thing could have happened to an atheist or a humanitarian. There was nothing overtly spiritual in my reaction, but I did have a very real sense of another and greater presence with me. It was a 'message' which came quite unbidden and totally unexpectedly.

Several years ago, we were going through a time of domestic upheaval concerning one of our children. We were facing what we knew was going to be a difficult and testing time. I felt anxious and depressed about what lay ahead.

I dreamed that I was climbing a very steep hill on a muddy path. Other people were with me but I couldn't identify them. At the top of the hill to the left was a line of beautiful autumn trees; at the right stood a huge lion on an outcrop of rock. I felt apprehensive, wanting to climb to the trees but being irresistibly drawn to the lion. As I approached the lion, he lunged towards me with his claws, but as he made contact with me he drew in his claws and embraced me - pushing me towards the trees.

I felt full of confidence and relief. The symbolism and significance of the dream is glaringly obvious. One hardly needs a dream analyst to unravel that one - but the feelings of relief and confidence with which I awoke were quite tremendous. It proved to be a turning point in our crisis and I really knew that however difficult things became, I would be able to cope, that something/one stronger than I would be there to guide, guard and support me. It was an intensely vivid dream and was an experience which started me on work with my dreams as a source of spiritual growth.

I KNOW PEOPLE WERE PRAYING

About five years ago, when cuts in the NHS and Welfare Benefits, plus increased military expenditure, were in the news, I felt a strong compulsion to take action personally. So I tried to divert money from the Inland Revenue to National Insurance and this entailed three Court appearances. I felt empowered and a sense of inward strength throughout this period. Even personal criticism directed towards me, and adverse comment in the Press, left me unmoved.

At a tragic (for me) time before and after my husband's death I felt a great sense of support, and I know people were praying for me.

FEELING OF BEING BROKEN

I had suffered severe emotional crises when my eldest son was born, and then again when he started school five years later. As a means of trying to relax I decided to try meditation.

I was surprised and at first alarmed (then later delighted) to discover a spiritual possibility from what had been intended as a relaxation technique. On one occasion of meditating, when I was feeling rather better than usual, I suddenly knew that 'love is the centre of the universe'.

It may sound strange put into words, and many might respond with a resounding 'So what?'. But the memory of the impact that this made on me and the accompanying excitement is still clear. I tried to tell one or two people who were close to me, but seemingly they could not understand the importance for me. Though mildly disappointed at this, I knew that the truth did not need to be corroborated, so it did not really matter.

Some months later I was hitting a bad patch and had been unable to arrange a meeting with a minister who had been helping me. I was alone in the house and in my neediness and desolation I let out a huge scream. I was surprised by a figure standing near. It was a Christ-like figure with his arms gently extended towards me, saying (or meaning), 'It's O.K., you're going to be O.K.'.

I knew that the Christ understood because he was made up of many small Picasso-like fragments, just like I felt. I do not believe that this was merely a hallucination because I was given the peace and strength to cope with the desolation which was still present, not psychologically denied. I understand the fragmented form to have been the best way in which the truth could be given considering the frame of mind that I was in at the time.

The whole experience lasted only a few minutes and at that time I had very little religious 'training' or explicit Christian beliefs, but like the other experiences the impact was powerful and lasting - at least in some measure.

Around this time I often longed to die, to be freed from my emotional pain. This longing was eased when I was at a neighbour's funeral. He was a young man who had died violently in an industrial accident. The church was packed and bright sunshine was flooding in through the altar window, so much so, that it almost seemed to blind me. Suddenly the light changed from being bright to being 'living' and I just 'knew' that it was not yet my time to die. I have still had fleeting death-wishes but, since then, never with the same power of either desire or fear.

My next significant religious experience was when I was

attending a Quaker conference for those in the caring professions. As a counsellor, I am often overworked and on this occasion I was tired beyond belief and, as usual, I was angry with myself for allowing myself to get so tired. I can no longer remember quite how it happened, except that I was in a large discussion group. I suddenly felt quite, quite broken. Although no one around noticed anything different, I felt that every cell in my body had fallen apart.

This feeling of being broken was accompanied by a distinct 'call': 'You are in the right place - now you must learn'. Although being a Friend was (and is) very important to me, I had no doubt that the reference to the 'right place' meant being a counsellor, and that what I must now learn was to manage the call/job in a healthy way.

Regrettably, I felt no one at Meeting could listen to me as I shared the impact of this experience. Fortunately I was able to speak with two counselling colleagues who were able to accept my emotions and also my spiritual understanding.

I HAND IT ALL TO YOU, LORD

One of my spiritual experiences involved the death of my aunt, just over three years ago. She had lived with us for about six years and was eight-five. She had a stroke and thrombosis in her stomach. The doctor said she would not live and gave her an injection of morphia for the pain.

Very kindly he said 'Be very careful what you say in this room. The hearing is the last sense to go and she will very likely hear until she dies, even though the morphia has made her unconscious'.

At a certain point I felt moved to read her the *Twenty-third Psalm*, so I read it to her. As I said 'Amen' she seemed to smile faintly and died. My cousin who was also in the room said 'I wouldn't have missed being here. There was such a wonderful peace in this room'.

On another occasion I visited the House of Commons as leader of a deputation seeking peace in the Korean war. I was confronted by my very belligerent MP and taken up a corridor on my own, with him shouting at me. As I walked along I silently prayed 'Lord, I don't know *how* to love this man. I hand it all to you, Lord'.

I don't know what exactly happened. All I know is he stopped shouting at me and I said 'I am a Christian Pacifist'. He said 'I've never met anyone like you before'. I didn't win him to seek a peaceful solution to the war, but at least we did have a peaceful conversation.

Another time a woman came and knocked at the door asking if she could stay for a while. We had three children. In different ways she was disruptive in the house, but I somehow felt I should look after her in spite of other people saying I should ask her to go.

In ministry at the Friends Meeting on Sunday I mentioned what was happening and asked if Friends would join me in praying for her. When I got home the lady said 'You've been praying for me, haven't you? Until now I've been so terribly afraid.' Strangely enough she vomited and vomited and vomited and said she didn't feel afraid any more.

I GOT MY MESSAGE

One Sunday I was feeling extremely ill in Meeting - a combination of 'nerves' and medication which was not having the desired effect - and for about fifteen minutes I prayed for a sense of the Divine Presence. I knew that such a sense would bring me relief, and my prayer was one of desperation. I felt nothing: there was simply nothing 'out there' nor in myself.

After that fifteen minutes or so my immediate neighbour stood up and said 'I feel very strongly a sense of the Spirit of God being present with us.' I got my message through him. I was not only grateful but healed.

A KIND OF ANGUISH

It was on the fifth day of an intensive silent retreat, learning Soto Zen meditation (simply sitting, facing a blank wall, allowing the mind to settle and clean). To my astonishment, the wall suddenly opened, like a ten-inch porthole. Through the opening I could see in a wonderful radiant colour and hear, in unusual vividness, a clear sparkling stream running over a stony bed. Bright sunlight filtered through willow trees overhanging the bank. I was immediately impressed with the heightened sensuousness, how real it was, not like something imagined.

I satisfied myself of this at the time by imagining another group of trees on the wall above the porthole. The difference was unmistakable. Understanding such an experience as a projection of my own mind in no way detracts from its lasting effect upon me as an experience of spiritual experience.

During an eight-day silent Zen retreat (said to make no concessions to Western weakness!) I was walking alone on an open hillside soon after dawn. Turning my head and looking across the valley I was greatly surprised and amazed to find myself weeping *and* laughing with feelings of tenderness and recognition and a kind of anguish at the marvel of what was happening. The landscape had not changed in appearance, but it was transfigured.

As an artist I am accustomed to seeing things form themselves into beautiful patterns and images; offering themselves as inspiration for paintings. This was quite another kind of beauty. I was no longer the observer seeing it. I was at one with it. I was it, and I recognised the experience as though I was remembering it. It aroused and returned what can only be named love.

It was as though all questions were answered. And the miracle of existence itself was not only revealed but possessed. I looked around at the muddy footpath, the stones on the path. I looked at the clouds and the overcast sky.

Everything was ordinary, how it always was, yet everything was transformed - inwardly. Outwardly the same, inwardly a radiance. Personal and impersonal, beyond words. And a thought which was more like a voice said 'Now I know all is well, I am satisfied and I am happy to die'.

Hold Her in the Light

I have now been married for thirty-six years and both my parents and in-laws are dead. About thirty years ago I was deeply troubled by my mother-in-law, a woman who caused pain and friction to all who came in contact with her. We lived far away and saw her but little, but the situation bothered me. At that time (I was staunch C of E) my husband and I knelt in prayer together each night and on one occasion I presented this problem.

I can only say that I felt wrapped in a warm glow of love - amazingly my husband was unaware of this - and an inner voice said, 'Think of her as your mother'. I tried, and failed miserably.

My own mother, whom I loved dearly and missed, had died when I was fifteen. I felt that I was being asked to replace her. I now understood the power of positive and negative thought and realize that I should have persevered in 'thinking', and even now hold her in the light.

A few years ago the inner voice told me to heal. I thought 'Oh no - not me'. The voice persisted and eventually I began in a White Eagle Absent Healing group.

COMMENT

These accounts of individual spiritual experience are virtually unclassifiable and even indefinable. Each is as vivid
and vital as spoken ministry in a good Meeting. We respond
as reader or listener in our own personal way, according to
our own 'condition'. We may be touched inwardly in the
spirit, or ministry may pass us by. It is as though writer
and reader, speaker and hearer need to be somehow in
tune if, in Matthew Arnold's phrase, 'the spark from
Heaven' is to fall.

Often there is an unmistakably numinous quality about
such communion, whether spoken or written, that defies
analysis. It is best nurtured in respectful silence and further
editorial comment would I think be out of place.

We come now to *Parts III* an *IV* and two further questions.
These are of a more direct kind. Both concern the relevance of
Quaker membership (or regular attendance) to religious
experience. How far is the Quaker form of worship appropriate as a source or context ?

ຂ

PART III

QUAKER
LINKS

Introduction to Part III

Replies to the remaining two questions presented little difficulty editorially since they deal with simpler issues of opinion. They form a supplement to the former replies and are not
concerned directly with religious or spiritual experience but
with attendance at Meeting for Worship and its relevance to
the inner aspect of the spiritual dimension.

Is being a Quaker conducive to this experience ? Is such
inner experience an integral part of being a Quaker or just a
chance characteristic for some members ?

Secondly, does Meeting for Worship adequately maintain
a right balance between inner and outer, general and individual aspects of religion ?

These are some of the concerns on which these replies
throw light, because they are based on experience and attendance at Meeting.

Replies to the Third Question

Is your own religious (or spiritual) experience specially linked to your being a Quaker (or Attender)? If so, please enlarge.

OUT OF STEP

I would logically expect a stray connection and yet, despite over twenty years of membership, I am still not sure that I *am* a Quaker; the more my inner life develops the more I seem to be out of step with the Meeting to which I belong. On the other hand I cannot conceive that I would have been content to be a member of a traditional Christian Church, to have no worshipping community to relate to ! As it is, the silent Meeting for Worship has allowed me to develop at my own pace and in my own way.

A PSYCHIC GIFT

Yes, indirectly. My spiritual development has been linked with individuals who were Quakers. Fifty years ago I met an Elder of the Quaker Meeting who had been trained in theology with a view to becoming ordained. He went to prison in the first World War and after his return became a Quaker and artist and did not pursue his first interest. He helped me enormously in my formative years.

Later, an American whom I met in India helped me by indicating a spiritual path which incorporated a psychic gift I have.

MUST BE INTERWOVEN

Yes, I believe my spiritual experience is linked to my being a Quaker - the two must be interwoven. The discipline of silence plus Quaker ways absorbed over the years create for me a firm foundation for spiritual search and understanding.

OUT OF THIS WORLD

No. Genuine religious experience is something 'out of this world', and consequently cannot be the result of belonging to any particular religious sect or denomination. The best example of this is St Paul's Damascus Road experience, which converted him from one faith to a completely different one.

MEDITATION

Through Quakers I came to know about and to take part in meditation, which I find rewarding.

THE ONLY LABEL

Yes, in so far as I came to Quakers as one who has at last *found*, rather than a refugee from Church of England or a Seeker. The ultimate vision, of course, is beyond labelling, which is why an Attender - who attends and pays attention - is the only label I can honestly accept. My Christianity includes Sufism and All Truth.

A WONDERFUL HOME-COMING

Yes, since joining two years ago. Being an elder and entering actively into the life of the meeting has quickened and consolidated my sense of living by the Spirit. The discovery of fellowship within a community of believers, aware of their spiritual life, is a wonderful home-coming after a lifetime of solitary journeying.

Rare and Nebulous

My experience, which is rare and nebulous, is not particularly linked with being a Quaker.

The Silence in Itself

No, my religious experience comes from being an Anglican for 84 years. I still keep that membership and find no conflict with my membership of Quakerism. I read theology at Cambridge and was ordained in 1932. After five years in parish work I became completely deaf and turned to work as a Chaplain to those deaf from birth, commonly known as the deaf and dumb. I have been retired for sixteen years.

I have for fifty years lived in complete silence. I hear not the loudest of sounds. Hence the silence in itself at Meeting is not of great importance.

It Could be That ...

I don't think my religious experience was specially linked to my being a Quaker, though it could be that my experience of Quaker Worship has fortified my 'practice of the presence of God', thereby making Him (Her) more accessible to me.

Before and Since

My spiritual experiences do not appear to be linked to my being a Quaker. They date both before and since my attendance and membership.

THE BEDROCK

My religious (spiritual) experiences are of course closely linked with my Quaker membership because Quaker worship has become a part of my daily life, after twenty-four years in the Society. Over the last few years, however, I have found spiritual nourishment in an increasingly wide range of circumstances/environments. For example, a recent week's visit to the community of Taizé in France gave me a tremendous spiritual uplift - worshipping with people with very different approaches to my own, in an ecclesiastical atmosphere which although very different from a Meeting for Worship contained the same deep, worshipful silences, and where music contributed greatly to the spirituality of worship services.

So I suppose the answer to the question might be that Yes, being a Quaker is the bedrock of my spiritual experience. But it is also a spring-board (sorry for the mixed metaphor) for other spirituality.

THE ROOT OF LIFE

I have read many writings on religion and life, understanding and discerned much to treasure in many, but always come back to Quaker witness as going down to the root of life experience.

CONFIRMATION

No. I was brought up in the Church of England. After confirmation I had a wonderful experience of being completely forgiven.

CONVINCEMENT

None of the experiences I have described are linked to my being a Quaker. On the other hand, they have not convinced me that I could be anything else but a Quaker.

DOES NOT REQUIRE ME

Yes, in the sense that the Quaker ethos turns on 'What canst *thou* say?' And does not require me to believe or experience what either the scriptures or a priest-figure or an established set of doctrine tells me to believe or to experience.

I came to Quakers about twenty-five years ago as an Attender and was accepted into membership about twelve years ago. Previous to that, I had gone through an Anglican school and regarded myself as Anglican until the end of my 'teens. I then had a flirtation with the Methodists for over ten years, but never joined either Church. In the end I rejected both because I could not believe what I was required to believe, though I had a very strong religious impulse most of the time. What is more, I saw a great discrepancy between the simplicity, poverty and lack of ceremony of Jesus of Nazareth on the one hand and the trappings and ceremonies in church buildings which were supposed to be there to worship him, on the other hand.

NOT SPECIALLY LINKED
No, my spiritual experiences are not specially linked to my membership of the Society of Friends.

A MEDIUM FOR GOD'S WORDS
Attending Meeting for Worship helps me in my spiritual experience/growth in various ways. It gives me time to listen to God - though of course I do this during the week, too. It enables me to hear God through other Friends' ministry, and gives me time to think about it. It also enables me, myself, to act as a medium for God's words (in ministry), which I regard as a spiritual experience. And it enables me to get to know and love other Friends in 'the things that are eternal', and to feel part of a spiritual family.

No
The answer, a little regretfully, has to be no.

UNWARRANTED, UNACCEPTABLE

This strikes me as a 'Have you stopped beating your wife?' type of question. There is an unwarranted, unacceptable assumption built into it.

Any experience, religious or other, will be a Quaker experience for me, in so far as I am a Quaker. I am tending to the view that *all* experiences are basically religious, since God is the only basic creator. A perfect Quaker sees God in everything all the time. Since I am not a perfect Quaker all my experiences are a mixture, which I have to be content to leave future experiences or events to comment upon.

Were the two Jews crucified with Christ having a Christian religious experience? Or a Jewish? We do not know if the hanging of Judas was his suicide or if he was executed by being 'suicided'. In either case was it a Zealot, Jewish or Christian experience?

One could perhaps ask was the sack of Jerusalem a Jewish religious experience? Or a Roman?

None of these experiences could be described as Quaker. But one can see their modern equivalents built into our modern lives.

I MADE THEM MY OWN

Being born into a Quaker family, regular Attender of Meeting for Worship and fully participant in the local meeting and in the life of the larger Society of Friends, I absorbed Quaker values in childhood. I made them my own as an adult. So my religious/spiritual experience is embedded in and nurtured by my membership of the Society of Friends.

I have had other kinds of religious/spiritual experience, e.g., in groups run by the Rev. Francis Dewar (a Spiritual Counsellor, author of *Live for a Change, Discovering and Using Your Gifts*) but even then, felt very much a Quaker in my responses.

Nature, music, beauty, poetry, love and friendship are other religious experiences for me, not necessarily linked to my being a Quaker.

HIGHER SELF

It is indeed linked to my being a Quaker. I feel that only in the Stillness and silence can I tune in to my 'Higher Self' and be aware of the presence of God.

AT LAST I KNEW

My first experiences of God came to me when I was an agnostic, having been brought up in an agnostic family. When at last I knew from direct spiritual experience that God was true, I had a great urge to share my new sensibilities with others. It took me fifteen years to find the Society of Friends and the fellowship of worship which I had been longing for.

FILLED WITH THE SOUND I LONG FOR

An *area* of my spiritual life is linked to attending Quaker meetings. I grew away from Catholicism because my questions seemed to raise a fear, a sort of dishonesty among those believers questioned. Total rejection, a long depression at the heart of which was a spiritual need.

That recognized, there followed another powerful need to share the search - but without dogma, without labels, without enforced joining-in. Quakers provided that. So I turn to Quakers for the stillness which, when deep, is filled with the sound I long for. They pin-point the listening as the heart of the spiritual experience, in a way no others quite do. And the few Quakers who dare to talk openly, outside the silence, of their experience answer the desperate need I have always felt, to share that reality: to be assured it was not just mine. I love the simplicity. It is God, and you and me.

But I should add that the core of my spiritual life is my own meditation, when I stop to ask 'What next?' and try, so inadequately, to listen.

COMMENT

What conclusions, if any, may be drawn from these replies to a relatively simple and direct query?

It would, I think, be fair comment to say that for these contributors spiritual experience certainly does arise within the Quaker context, though not exclusively. Some mention the sharing with others in worship, the silence and stillness, the simplicity and generally meditative atmosphere - all these being conducive to religious experience. They are certainly characteristic of Quaker ways and worship and to that extent may be regarded as 'specially linked' to being a Quaker or Attender.

There are also those who find spiritual experience is not limited to Quaker membership although consistent with it, for instance the experience of music, nature and membership of other denominations or religions.

Among these replies there is no charismatic, sectarian claim that for these contributors spiritual experience is exclusive to membership. They do perhaps suggest that Quaker worship and membership form a natural background to spiritual experience, at least for them.

ౚ

PART IV

THE RELEVANCE OF QUAKER WORSHIP

Replies to the Fourth Question

Does Meeting for Worship encourage or discourage, help or hinder you, in relation to religious (or spiritual) experience?

GENERALLY UNENTHUSIASTIC

The general ethos of our meeting seems generally unenthusiastic about spiritual experience, but as it is something we don't discuss it is difficult to be certain. Those of us for whom it appears to be both a natural occurrence and a necessity are neither encouraged nor helped by the meeting in general. There is a mild feeling of discouragement and the hint that our energies would be better employed in more extrovert activities.

We do, however, support each other, and we have the silence. Finding my own way into this has been, in the course of the years, both educative and transformative. In addition to support from individual Friends I have been grateful for the encouragement and fellowship offered in the Open Letter Movement.

DISCOURAGES AND HINDERS

My attitude to this is best expressed by the fact that I am a member of the Friends Fellowship of Healing, the Alastair Hardy Research Centre, the Churches Fellowship for Psychical and Spiritual Studies. Apart from one or two members of our meeting I would not feel much sympathy and therefore I think the meeting discourages and hinders my more mystical approach to religious experience.

A Vital Part of My Journey

The Meeting for Worship over the years has at times encouraged me and at others discouraged, because I have felt that my ministry does not always express what I had intended to convey or does not spring from that of God within me, but from a lower source. Self-recriminations then take over for the rest of the day. I also find it difficult not to criticise other ministry. Maybe this is all a vital part of my journey towards self-knowledge and spiritual experience.

Deepens One's Awareness

Attending Meeting for Worship does help spiritual experience, only that it deepens one's awareness and sensitivity. One is able to reflect on ministry. Rarely and specially the 'Spirit of God' is very present.

Much-Needed Comfort

For me religious experience in Meeting for Worship may happen in two ways. There is the wonderful sense that comes sometimes in the silence of a 'gathered meeting' of being surrounded by peace and love - 'When two or three are gathered together in my name, there also am I'.

Then there are occasions during meeting when a Friend's ministry speaks directly to my condition, answering perhaps a deep inner question, or providing much-needed comfort and hope or enlightenment. I know many Friends share this experience.

Not Keenly Aware

I am not keenly aware of its help in regard to religious experience, except perhaps for the 'stillness' gained.

ALWAYS HELPFUL

Attending Quaker Meeting most certainly does not discourage or hinder religious or spiritual experience. Of course some meetings are better than others but a quiet period of thought is always helpful, even if the meeting is not a gathered one.

I personally always appreciate a short vocal offering near the beginning to focus one's thoughts, whether it leads to further ministry or not. In fact - dare I say it? - I sometimes wish we had a theme for each Sunday, like the Church Calendar but much more flexible and topical !

SUNS OF GOD

Simply, the more Love there is, sharing Love, the more wonderful life is. Meetings vary greatly with those present, just as silence can be dead or utterly living. A living silence is w/holy (*sic*) creative - even though no word be spoken, while even a 'dead' silence can be profitable as a discipline or time for self-examination. Anyone who has experienced 'being in the Light' perforce longs for the experience to be repeated, for only then do we *know* ourselves to be the Sons (Suns) of God !

PURITY AND UNIVERSALITY OF STILLNESS

Encourages and helps. Meeting for Worship provides the occasion for focus of one's conscious and unconscious energies. Being a *shared* experience adds a - perhaps *the* - most significant dimension. It is a moving experience to sense the purity and universality of stillness and silence as worship.

TELEPATHIC, COINCIDENTAL TOGETHERNESS

I find Meeting for Worship is particularly uplifting as regards making me more sensitive to 'leadings of the Spirit' in everyday life and to the feelings of others in the Meeting. I am particularly impressed by the 'telepathic', 'coincidental togetherness' thinking and feeling in the Meeting which is evidenced by the ministry.

ACTS OF PRAISE

Attending Quaker Meeting has helped me. It is of course not specially new to me as in the past I have attended Anglican retreats when silence has been kept strictly over a period of two or even three full days.

But the regular Sunday Quaker Meeting has made me consider more carefully the thought processes during the hour of silence and compare them with worship in the ordinary church, e.g. the sense of 'awe' and acts of 'praise' seem to be given far less value than in the ordinary church. Neither of them appears in the index of *Christian Faith and Practice*.

DANGEROUS BUT NECESSARY

It greatly helps me. It is now autumn, I can see again birds lining up on the telephone wires, waiting to migrate. No doubt they also feel the need for like-minded company on being faced with a pending great endeavour, compelling, dangerous but necessary for them. Faced as we are with the built-in necessity to overcome what George Fox saw as an ocean of spiritual darkness with moving into and indeed providing Christ's ocean of spiritual light, we can and should help and comfort one another. Meeting for Worship does this for me. But perhaps this is because I was born and brought up in the Quaker tradition.

FEEL UNSUPPORTED BY MY MEETING

I believe that my spiritual experiences come from outside of me and so Meeting for Worship is not relevant, though my openness may be.

My openness is made easier by some Meetings for Worship, but also by many other life experiences - mostly connected with nature.

I do feel unsupported by my Meeting in relation to spiritual experience, as with deeply-felt emotions. I would like to feel freer to speak openly of these experiences which are very important to me. I don't take many risks in sharing anything beyond the comfortable norms of our well-heeled community. The few times I have spoken, I have met with a polite but superficial reception - no empathy, little imagination or even interest.

I regret this, as we all lose the opportunity of a richer life together.

GROWTH OF THE SPIRITUAL DIMENSION

Meeting for Worship, *when I have prepared properly for it* (which I find to be the essential criterion for success) certainly encourages and helps my spiritual growth. This growth may not often include spiritual happenings, revelations or experiences in the sense of your original query, but is a slow (very slow) growth of the spiritual dimension of my personality.

OUR RELATIONSHIPS WITH OTHERS

Religious experience does depend so much on our relationships with others, so Meeting for Worship, wherever I am able to attend, is an imperative for me. Spiritual experience depends more on my own meditations.

I PRAY FOR GUIDANCE

I find this very difficult. Sometimes I feel encouraged - sometimes discouraged. I believe that Jesus is with us now, in Meeting and personally if we desire Him. Also I believe God loves us all and that the spirit of Jesus can move us whoever we are. Sometimes I think Friends are too tolerant in their approach - and then I think maybe I am not tolerant enough. I pray for guidance.

THE MOST FAVOURABLE ATMOSPHERE

I have always felt that I had my own part to play in helping a Meeting for Worship to come to life. Apart from the rare 'spiritual experiences' that occur unexpectedly in unfamiliar places or on special occasions (e.g. when listening to classical music), I find in the Quaker Meeting for Worship the most favourable atmosphere for the renewal or strengthening of the life of the spirit.

I LONG TO SIT IN THE UPPER ROOM

This question is very hard indeed to answer. On the one hand it *must* help, because I feel drawn back week after week, and when I can't go, I feel deprived and unsettled. Certainly, at the end of Meeting for Worship, I feel tranquillised, relaxed and fortified for the coming week. Quite often, I have been able to let the matters which make a turmoil in my mind fall into some sort of proportion. I also value the fact that everyone else in the room has been engaged in approximately the same exercise.

But too often, I come away with a great spiritual thirst unslaked. Instead of being tranquillised, I long to be inspired, electrified, transported, empowered. I long to sit in the equivalent of that 'upper room' at Pentecost and feel the Spirit descend upon us all and transform us. I long to hear a latter-day George Fox say the magic words that unlock the spirit.

Very often, the ministry is interesting and valuable, but it is nearly always philosophical or educational rather than strictly spiritual. In our Meeting, the great bulk of ministry falls on three or four people, with just the occasional very welcome contribution from someone else. Occasionally, someone who is nearly always silent gets up and says something inspirational and I value it very much. I only wish that such Friends would speak more often. Sometimes, uncertainty or over-modesty or undue self-effacement keeps members on their seats when the Spirit is prompting away at them to no avail ! I am convinced of this.

I am not one of those who want a great deal of ministry in any one Meeting; silence should always be the stuff of Quaker worship. However, I do like *some* ministry, and I do like varied ministry.

Incidentally, I think that there is some self-delusion among Friends. Sometimes the silent Meeting is profoundly worshipful, but sometimes it jolly well isn't - and I fancy I can feel the difference. But is that self-delusion, too ?

AWARENESS OF THE TRANSCENDENT

This is difficult to answer. In Meeting for Worship I find nothing which seems to encourage growth in the kind of mindfulness to which I refer in my answer to Question 1 (*Deaths ... lead to life ?* page 25). As I indicated there, such an approach to daily life for me affords the essential religious (or spiritual) experience, one that I foster periodically by an actively sought awareness of the transcendent and eternal in the earthy and contemporary.

MY INNER SPRINGS OF LIFE

Quaker Meeting for Worship is a great help and encourage-ment to me in my religious/spiritual life. If, during the week, I have felt spiritual dryness or moods of unbelief, the power present in a Meeting for Worship will usually freshen my inner springs of life and renew my beliefs.

It is my closest experience of 'God', of communion with the Holy Spirit and with the same spirit in fellow worshippers drawing us closer together at a deep level. And I do experience, by the end of Meeting for Worship, 'the evil in me weakened and the good raised up'.

If, through choice or lack of opportunity, I neglect attendance at Meeting, I definitely feel the *lack* of all these influences.

'ALL SHALL BE WELL ...'

I am definitely encouraged and helped. The communal worship which can sometimes reach to wonderful depths sends me away with spiritual batteries recharged and an additional awareness of being part of this world and, indeed, the next. I can better cope with the ever-present violence which exists, and am better able to believe that 'All shall be well and all manner of things shall be well'.

A HEAVENLY BALM

I find that in Quaker Meeting for Worship the sense of stillness that descends upon the soul is a heavenly balm which spreads upon all present where faithfulness and the love of God meet. Hence it is a 'Meeting' in the best sense of the word, where living communion takes place. This may be helped or hindered by vocal contributions depending on the sensibilities and receptivity of the worshippers.

SOMETHING IRRESISTIBLE DETERMINING HOW I ACT

Primarily Quaker worship encourages me in that so often I find ministry homes-in on 'my condition'. I have had the most extraordinary experiences at Meeting - that awful pounding heart and inability to breathe and a sense of being forced into horribly emotional speech. Afterwards, I feel wrung-out and disorientated and am not sure what good it does anyone, or me. I was about to say the embarrassment I often feel makes it a discouraging experience, but that's not the whole of it. Afterwards, there is a depth of peace.

Sometimes I have felt the same turmoil elsewhere, of being taken over, something irresistible determining how I act. Afterwards that same peace, knowing it was right. Always the action was unlike anything *I* would dream up.

I do notice that when I am spiritually fog-bound I don't go to Meeting. Often it's when I am on the run, so there must be something too painfully illuminating about Meeting which would help, but which I often avoid.

After many meetings I feel very vulnerable, very exposed and the social chit-chat afterwards I can't cope with. It's too savage a switch of mode. So that is a hindrance.

In the silence of Meeting I feel at one with Quakers. In the hubbub of massed Quakers, in social and practical roles, I feel inadequate. I don't *do* or *join* in the way Quakers do and that is a dichotomy I find very difficult and a hindrance. I have not found the bridge between contemplative and active Quakerdom.

CAUGHT UP IN A FORCE-FIELD

To me, Questions 3 and 4 are much the same, as Meeting for Worship is so central.

What Meeting for Worship means to me goes back to the very first Meeting I attended, five years ago. Before then I had been meditating privately for five years, in a rather haphazard way. During that time, I had discovered that what I had been seeking was there all along - namely a sense of oneness with something indefinable. It was not a matter of seeking, but of being open to what was there already.

Meeting unexpectedly added a new dimension. Almost the moment I sat down I was aware of a gathered sense - of a shared communion. This I had never felt before - not even in group meditations. It was as though I was caught up in a force-field that was greater than I was, although I too formed part of it, and different from the sense of communion found in private meditation.

That shared sense has remained with me ever since. Of course it varies from meeting to meeting; sometimes there are no more than flashes or glimpses: at others the sense of being held is there from the beginning and time has no meaning.

Meeting, at its best, is an encounter with that of God in all present. Subtly, I believe we carry that unspoken awareness with us into daily life, in the form of heightened compassion and social action. We do so not out of any hope for reward, or sense of do-gooding, but because the shared spiritual awareness of the silence and the creativity of ministry leave a heightened sense of awareness of our fellow human beings. Often, we ourselves may be all but unaware of this; but in my own mind I have no doubt about the link between the mystical communion of the shared silence and the social concern that has been so characteristic of Quakerism down the ages.

COMMENT

Unlike the first two questions, the last two are concerned with generalities rather than individual experience - with outer, practical aspects rather than inner.

The contributors differ in the way they see membership and the way Quaker Meeting for Worship affects their spiritual life - and in how their fellow worshippers affect them, too. It is simple to list positive and negative criticisms, to give something of a general view as sought by the two questions. The following comments are taken directly from the replies and most of them are quotations.

Positive Criticism

Some contributors derive comfort, peace, joy, love and help from Meeting and from their membership. There is a 'living sense of oneness'. The silence may be experienced as 'living', enhancing the 'growth of the spiritual dimension'. The quiet stillness is relaxing and tranquillizing or, positively, uplifting and enlightening or even creative.

Thus Meeting provides a 'favourable atmosphere for renewal and strengthening'. For some, Meeting feels a homecoming, in its togetherness and shared experience as 'part of the spiritual family'. It may be a bedrock, 'the root of life experience' or a 'recharging of the spiritual batteries.'

Some speak of Meeting in direct religious terms, as the presence of God or of Jesus, an experience of or encounter with the Holy Spirit; as transcendence or listening to God, as a mystical union or an affirmation that 'God loves us'.

The ministry of other worshippers may be helpful, coming from 'that of God' within them. Even when not spiritual, ministry may encourage reflection.

Negative Criticism

Meeting may prove discouraging and the silence is sometimes 'dead'. It may hinder spiritual experience and give one an impression of being out-of-step and spiritually unsupported. Ministry may be unrelated to spiritual experience, leaving one's 'spiritual thirst unslaked'. The spirit of God may be missing so that ministry is tranquillizing but not inspiring. One found in fellow members a lack of sympathy with anything deeply felt and a lack of enthusiasm about spiritual matters, an interest only in practical affairs.

These contrasts may be seen and felt as conflicts or as signs of vitality and variety, evidence of seeking rather than errors, as arising from differences of temperament rather than from wrong-headedness. This may seem over-optimistic to anyone who has a sense of alienation or lack of sympathy. A union of opposites (of whatever kind) is usually difficult and often daunting, especially on issues that are felt to be vital. Yet it is a characteristic of the Quaker way. One contributor refers to 'the link between mystical communion of the shared silence and social concern that has been so characteristic of Quakerism down the ages' - that is to say, harmony and not a discord of opposites, - between the outer and the inner, the practical and the spiritual.

Another contributor refers to 'an actively sought awareness of the transcendent and eternal in the earthy and temporary', words that might be used for any truly gathered Meeting at its best: the transcendent *in* (not against) the earthy, the eternal *in* (not against) the temporary. This is a tension but not a conflict and it is positive, constructive and may be even creative. Good works need inspiration from the spirit; inspiration needs to be expressed constructively and with goodwill. This is the dynamic of Quaker living, a tense and sometimes painful but constructive tension.

The quiet, low-key poem that now brings this enquiry to an end acknowledges in its modest way and on a modest scale the differences between inner and outer concerns that can divide or inspire us. It was sent in response to this project and surely captures the spirit of a good Meeting.

QUAKER SILENCE

The room is quiet
The flowers say 'peace'.
Outside the window
The world goes on. We hear
Noises of cars, birds sing,
Wind blows.
Only ourselves
Inside are stilled.
The clamour of our minds
Is stilled,
We attend
We wait.

And like the returning tide
Gentling the shore
His presence
Renders us true.
Whether out loud in words
Or in our thoughts only,
Our lives and concerns
Come into His light,
And the strands of thought
Of all the minds
Are gathered to Him.
And the concerns of all the hearts

Are His concerns.
His presence holds
Contains and blesses,
Drawing out truth
Informing with love.

There is a timelessness
Broken now by
A rustling sound
At the hour's close
When hand meets hand,
Symbol of the love
Enjoined upon His Friends.
And eyes look out
From hearts where Truth
Has found a home.
One's loath to leave
The beauty of this grace
For mundane things.

JENNY DIXON

ဈ

Appendices

Appendix A

DESCRIPTIVE NOTES SENT TO ENQUIRERS

Religious Experience - A Quaker Enquiry

In a recent article in *The Friend* readers were invited to ask for details of a possible small-scale enquiry. These notes outline the present suggestions (which may be amended according to the response).

Background
The work of the Alister Hardy Research Centre has been the subject of two recent books reviewed in *The Friend*. It was based on the religious experience of a large number of contributors who wrote in answer to wide public advertisement and publicity.

This research revealed a curious fact. Religious experience seems to be so common as to be quite normal and yet it is so private that most correspondents had never told anyone about it. All of them were describing their own personal religious (or spiritual) experience, though they were not all members of any particular religion or denomination. (Some may have been Friends.)

It struck some of us that there might well be a useful Quaker contribution to the same general topic, based on our understanding of the religious life and our particular way of worship. Among Quakers there is an enduring interest in historical, moral, theological, universal and actively practical aspects of religion. But there is an inner spiritual basis that inspires all this - the Inner Light or the Inner Voice. To Quakers, it is this which makes the Society of Friends a religious community rather than a secular, charitable organisation.

Perhaps we (like so many of the AHRC contributors) feel the same stress between what is widespread and yet so private and personal that we hesitate to talk about it. In Meeting for Worship we sometimes recognise an experience of the Inner Light or the Inner Voice or the promptings of God. We may share it, or share in it. But it is hard to describe, explain or define it.

Such experiences can occur in ordinary daily life, at work or play, alone or with others, in nature or works of art. They often seem without identifiable stimulus or cause. Although hard to explain, these experiences carry a conviction that is authentic. It is this aspect of experience that the present venture seeks to illuminate. It will be based on what has actually happened to Friends or Attenders (within Meeting or independently). Perhaps 'spiritual' is a better word than 'religious' for these experiences.

Aim
This will not be a large-scale research project based on replies to pre-set questions to be analysed or classified. The aim is to understand and share religious experience in all its uniqueness and variety. Detailed questionnaires will not be used nor shall we seek statistical information (age, sex, occupation etc.). Friends are invited to describe their experience as naturally and freely as they find most congenial.

Method
Now to be more personal. If you would like to take part, you are asked to consider the following:

1 Writing and sending to me (in as much detail as you wish) your answer to this general question:

From your own personal experience, what do you understand by religious (or spiritual) Experience ?

(In other words, what does the expression mean to you, not in theory or doctrine but in your own life? 'What canst *thou* say?' Please write naturally, as in a letter to a friend, not formally).

2 Writing and sending to me (separately) a reply to this second question:
Can you describe a religious (or spiritual) experience that has happened to yourself (more than one if you like) ?

(The more detail the better, such as the circumstances, what happened, how it affected you, how it arose, what resulted from it; these are offered not as questions to be answered in turn. They are just suggestions for the ground you may like to cover).

3 Nothing you reply to the enquiry will be printed without your permission. It can be anonymous if you wish.
If editing or shortening is necessary, you will be invited to approve the edited version.

4 At this early stage it is not possible to say how much or how little material can eventually be included. That must depend on the response. A few detailed replies would be more helpful than a lot of brief ones.

5 If you know any Friend or Attender who would like to take part in this enquiry, would you please show them these notes so they, too, can write.

6 If you would like to make further suggestions before you reply fully, please do send them. They will be gratefully considered.

Finally

I am writing to you as the individual collator or editor. But I have the support of a small group who have relevant experience and expertise and who have kindly agreed to advise on all aspects of this venture, though I must take responsibility for its final form. It is still at a tentative and exploratory stage because its final form must depend on what response is forthcoming.

Please accept advance thanks for any help you are willing to give. And please excuse me from an immediate and purely formal acknowledgement. It may take quite a time before I can reply properly.

Appendix B

EDITORIAL FOOTNOTE

Editing an enquiry such as this involves three major responsibilities, to the contributors, to potential readers and to the final form and scope of the publication. These sometimes overlap and may conflict.

The basis of this project is personal experience of each contributor. At the outset it was decided to frame a few open-ended questions that would be clear and stimulating without influencing replies. Draft explanatory notes incorporating the first two questions were considered by members of the Support Group. They did not meet to discuss the draft but each wrote comments and suggestions as appropriate. Fifty-three Friends or Attenders asked for a copy and about half took part in the enquiry. (The agreed version of the notes is reprinted as Appendix A.)

Some replies to the first question strayed into accounts of personal belief or general theory. These had to be pruned to keep to the point of the question. No reply was condensed or re-written but some are extracts from what was submitted. A compromise had to be made between the three responsibilities, to reader, contributor and publication.

Replies to the second question were mostly longer and more detailed; they form the heart of the project. In a few instances I felt obliged to omit part (or occasionally the whole) of a reply because the events described were not religious (or spiritual) in any ordinary, generally-accepted sense. I owed it to the writers not to be too ruthless in my pruning. I trust I have erred on the side of leniency rather than stringency. The amount of space that could be given to the replies had also to be considered and allocated.

Whether contributions were to be anonymous or attributed was a difficult decision. Some contributors insisted on anonymity, most of them voiced no preferences and one wanted all to be attributed. It seemed right to have the same rule for all and that meant being anonymous. I was also influenced by the fact that the enquiry was not intended as a study of personalities (like case histories or biographies) but a mosaic of experiences.

The final order of the replies was decided chiefly on the same principle and also to help readers to form their own assessment of the nature and value and relevance for themselves of the experience of others. This was necessarily a question of editorial judgment and feeling. I can but appeal to the tolerance of any contributor who is dissatisfied with it.

Replies to the last two questions cover the connection or relevance between religious experience and being a Quaker. The Quaker way of worship may be the natural result of religious experience or it may be the direct avenue to it.

These last two questions were sent out a month or two after the original two. The replies show how the individual contributors see this connection, if for them there is one. As before, the order of printing is not the same in each section.

Finally, there is an overall responsibility of a different kind. This is to avoid, so far as possible, any intrusion of an editor's own religious or spiritual values, views or beliefs into the editorial function. I cannot judge success or failure in this, but I do proclaim the intention.

Appendix C

SUGGESTED FURTHER READING ON SPIRITUAL EXPERIENCE

QUAKER BOOKS

Signs of Life, J. Ormerod Greenwood
The Creative Imagination, Kenneth Barnes
Encounter with Silence, John Punshon
The Sense of Glory, Ralph Hetherington
An Exercise of the Spirit, Anne Hosking and others
Where Words Come From, Douglas V Steere
Courage to Grow, Ruth Fawell. Quaker Home Service

FROM OTHER TRADITIONS

Mysticism, Evelyn Underhill. Methuen
The Varieties of Religious Experience, William James. Fount, Collins
The Choice is Always Ours, Dorothy Berkley Philips etc. Harper-Collins
How to Meditate, Lawrence Le Shan. Turnstone Press
A Dazzling Darkness, Patrick Grant. Fount, Collins
The English Mystics of the 14th Century, Karen Armstrong. Kyle Cathie
The Way of Transcendence, Alistair Kee. SCM
Solitude, Anthony Storr. Fontana
The River Within, Christopher Bryant. Longman & Todd
Religious Experience Today, David Hay. Mowbray
Exploring Inner Space, David Hay. Mowbray
Discovering God Within, John R Yungblutt. Element

Index of Entries